WRITERS REPUBLIC

Head & Heart

A Journey Inward

IZZY IS REAL

WRITERS REPUBLIC L.L.C.
515 Summit Ave. Unit R1
Union City, NJ 07087, USA

Website: *www.writersrepublic.com*
Hotline:*1-877-656-6838*
Email: *info@writersrepublic.com*

Ordering Information:
Quantity sales. Special discounts are available on quantity purchases by corporations, associations, and others. For details, contact the publisher at the address above.

Library of Congress Control Number: 2021935474
ISBN-13:   978-1-64620-676-6   [Paperback Edition]
                978-1-63728-468-1   [Hardback Edition]
                978-1-64620-677-3   [Digital Edition]

Rev. date: 04/08/2021

Contents

To God I give glory for my trials, tribulations, and triumphs. To my family I am forever indebted. To friends, supporters, and fans I am forever grateful. To those I have had the pleasure of rubbing shoulders with throughout my life, I appreciate you for your existence. It is an honor to be alive... even in 2020.

Park Day

Is it too soon to say I miss you?

I have no more words to fill this page

I spent them all on the FaceTime call we had last night

The one where you asked me questions

I took them as interrogation and you spoke them without holding back vulnerability

Your words spilled out in a rush with a soft force that rocked me as it reached my conscious

My soul heard everything you didn't say and caught every whiff of doubt, smoke screening the parts of you not many have seen

But yet you still want to show me

Let me in

Hold me

Let me know what it is you need from me

I

I am here

I don't know why but I know something in me is changing

Something in you is changing

I'm scared

Not of you but of how fast things are changing

Your walls

Have been no more than an invisible fence with the collar around your heart reminding it of what happens when it runs away

Not from you out of fear but out of curiosity and love of all things new

It's hard for you to bare the thought of losing her again

She knows the good visitors from bad and never really barks or bite unless provoked to roll or sit like she's some animal

No, your little girl has spunk

She has class

Witt

Spice

Vigor

D-R-ive

Intelligence

Resilience

And play

My little guy, my heart named Izzy, loves seeing yours at that one park we met at down the street called Conversation

Yea, he goes crazy and always knows when he's about to see her

But sometimes she doesn't want to play

As our lips move and dance with each sentence shortly following with a laugh or smirk

My heart looks at me

Where he usually waits for my okay he leaves my side at the first sight of you

Chasing your heart in the fields as we sit on the bench...perplexed at how quickly our pups made friends

Your's dipping and dodging keeping my little guy off your heels

"She's too quick" I mention to you as we watch

He never actually catches her, but he can

He's fast enough, but he's scared

Scared that maybe she doesn't want to get caught

If she bites he'll be spooked

Or if he catches her she, what if she doesn't want to play anymore

That would make him not want to play anymore

Rejection to him is a splinter in the paw

A cut to the heart

Causing our conversation to stop and a womb to be treated...behind the invisible fences...in the comfort of privacy and retracting

D' naltrop lane and Aksala pnt. are just spoken words away from each other

Neighboring streets joining at the same church...where our spirits met

I'm at home thinking of you

Pondering the question if there would ever be a day I get tired of seeing you, hearing from you, speaking to you

That thought scares me

I don't know the future

And I'm still getting to know you

The real you

We stopped playing our highlight reels for each other a long time ago

Three weeks ago actually

When we had our first date?(question mark)

That's neither here nor there but the point is...I find it awkward that I miss you... this much

Like, the type of miss you where I layed in bed all day and didn't want to talk to anyone because I only wanted to talk to you kind of miss you

Like, the distract myself with Netflix, Instagram, and quarantining because in 2020 right now it's day 3 and I give two shits because I'm not talking to you type of miss you

Like the...okay Imma stop while I'm ahead because you get the point

P.S. (Also known as a sidebar)

Turns out there was never a
splinter btw

In my heart's paw

Just a bruised spirit

My little guy can be quite
sensitive sometimes

When he heard your girl
bark he thought he hurt her

He didn't mean to

But I think he's good now

He hasn't stopped panting,
pacing, howling, and
waiting for the day

That day

The next day

Conversation in the
park day

Touch

Touch, a connecting point when touching another's skin

Touch, the gateway drug to intimacy leaving you one day strung out on love

Touch, the first ripple of a wave that sways your soul as it rides the vibrations of trust

Touch, you have to be close enough to engage and loved enough for its accepted continuation

Touch, it locks you into the physical database of another's memory

We learn the rules of good touching and bad touching at a young age

I learned

I learned what was socially appropriate

That there's a different way to touch a girl than to touch a boy

Hug a girl and fist pound a boy

Hold hands with a girl and give ya boy a shoulder check

Older translation meant give a girl flirtation and give a guy a joke

Give a girl a kiss, and give a guy a head nod

Give a woman sex, and give a man companionship

No homo, cuz you know, I can't be gay

I swear I'm not gay, I like women, I can prove it

I don't like how guys hands feel on me intimately

Once I got older I learned that touch can tap into memories

My body remembers more than I've allowed my mind to

My body was betrayed and to protect the perpetrator I then betrayed myself

Israel don't think about it

There's nothing wrong with you

You let it happen

What if you liked it

Just protect them

Snitches get stitches

I was four then I was nine, man it's crazy how time flies when you're having fun, keeping secrets, getting candy for every mission uncompromised, that's when I learned to run

Run from the pain

Run from the memories

Run from the confusion

Israel run

It didn't happen

Israel no one touched you

It's normal to forget your childhood

Everyone forgets the bad in their childhood, just don't tell anyone you've forgotten it all

Israel, you might have blocked memories

Like the one that resurfaced twelve years later after you lost the one you loved

Not to death but to prosecution

I was twelve years a slave to my own mind and my body five years a slave to welcomed touch

I grew up thinking nothing happened to me

Always asking God why my life had no pain

Believing that I was unscathed by any childhood stories filled with trauma or regret

Then I started noticing

Noticing that I always put others first

Think of everyone else before myself

It was the mask of Christian moral with a broken face of self-neglect

Where did this behavior begin?

It began when a nine-year-old boy decided that he would stay strong for a broken family of seven that had just watched a loved one walk away

With untold secrets and unaddressed turmoil in my heart, I no longer cried, but let the tails of my tears dry on my face

Like pillars, they stood tall crusting with age and maturity like those of the Parthenon

These pillars were proof that I could be the one to lean on

My siblings were safe, because I, the middle of five, had concluded that they were to be priority number one

Because Israel, was fine

Israel had no untold secrets, no unaddressed turmoil, no memories of any pain outside of that which he saw in his brother and sisters eyes

That's when it started

That's when Israel taught himself how to forget about himself

To survive

To cope

To cope, with the pain

I grew up in church, but we never talked about this

The pain caused by touch

As a teenager I started to think something was wrong with me

Wondering, asking myself what went wrong

Wondering why I couldn't stop the horniness

Wondering, why I wanted so much to be in the arms of someone who loved me, someone who, touched me

My dad was present but I was distant

All I knew from him was corrective discipline

Not tenderness

The only tenderness I trusted was from a woman

As a young man detached sex was easy

Because it's easy to be affectionate, it's hard to love

The only way to love others is to love yourself first

An ex taught me that

I never trusted someone so much before, nor had I ever had someone show me how to love myself

They say love is blind, I say affection is and true love looks back at you in the mirror

I've been upset with myself

I've hated myself for so long because I betrayed myself

I stayed silent...just like a touch in the dark

The type of touch that comes with a whisper in the night behind closed doors warranting for quiet, secret, tumultuous pleasure

I told myself that getting touched was okay, as long as it was by someone I loved

And I loved my big brother, I loved him very much

Thank God...
Question Mark?

Frantically evading my feelings as if tears would make an EpiPen closely follow

I'm allergic to recognizing pain

Suppression is my one pack a day, I guess this addiction is hereditary

I've locked off parts of myself to keep myself out

I still think about her

I still miss her

I often think about how she's doing

If she's talking to someone new

I know there's no longer a chance for us but I can feel her still

She's lodged between my rib cage like steak in my back teeth

I've never hated flossing until now

But at least I'm full

Stuffed

Bloated with memories of when things were better

When we were happy

When I was happy

They say I'm too hard on myself...my family and friends

They tell me I need to give myself a break

I used to cry myself to sleep because of giving my heart away too soon

People visiting my heart
as if I'm some Black Friday
discount

"Get more for less"

I just smile

I guess it's true

I need to heighten my
security

Need a strict no return
policy

You won't get to open
and use my heart only to
return it beaten, bruised,
dismembered, and misused
in between 30 days

That's not what she did

Which is the very thing
fucking me up

She loved me, with the
purest love

I wanna say I've moved on

I've tried to physically but to
no avail

I don't love easy but it's not a
bad thing to try again is it?

What if love just falls in
your lap again

Is it love?

Where's the line between
wisdom and taking a leap of
faith

Should there even be a line?

This is why they say I think
too much

So I guess that means I just
jump

Jumping back in time I find
the moment I chose wrong

I laid in bed crying my eyes
to sleep just to forget it all

I loved her still, but my love
for her could no longer be
the love she deserved so I
stuffed

I stuffed the love I had
for her and myself and
pondered

Prodded

No, plotted

Exchanged my love for lust
and took off

I needed to forget and
remind myself that I
couldn't love the one I had
given my all to

With every shedded article
of clothing from every

lust-filled night I pushed, pressed, and suppressed my feelings

Because they couldn't exist

Something's gotta give

It was either me or my emotions

I figured suicide wasn't a great choice so I chose my emotions

Terrible odds to work with but I chose life, so thank you God...question mark?

We have an interesting relationship

God and I

I do what I know is right and often feel punished for my obedience

It sometimes feels like a sick game where I go against every grain of what I want to do in order to do that thing

THE RIGHT THING

It's cost me so so much

I often say, "Regretting anything you've done in your life is regretting a part of yourself. The art of living is accepting yourself to love yourself."

But that's easy to say

Doing is another and I fucking hate myself sometimes

I feel like I heard a few audible gasps in this cold empty room at 5:30 in the morning

I always think about how much life I have left to live and I don't know if gives me hope or anxiety

I hope one day to find myself and be happy with myself...with all of myself

Then anxiety reminds me of all the hurt that has brought me to my current state and lovingly reminds me that with growth there is pain

Hope holds more power than we think and fear can if we allow it

Fear will make us believe anything

Because I'm still trying not to believe I've walked away

from the very thing I've always wanted

I don't want to believe I've made the wrong choice and I'm afraid I'm not confident that I did

That was 5 months ago

I don't expect to have fully moved on after the best year of my life

But I know that living in the past means either I haven't addressed the pain or I'm overthinking it

Either way, all I know is this shit better make sense one day cuz I'm tired of reaching for EpiPens

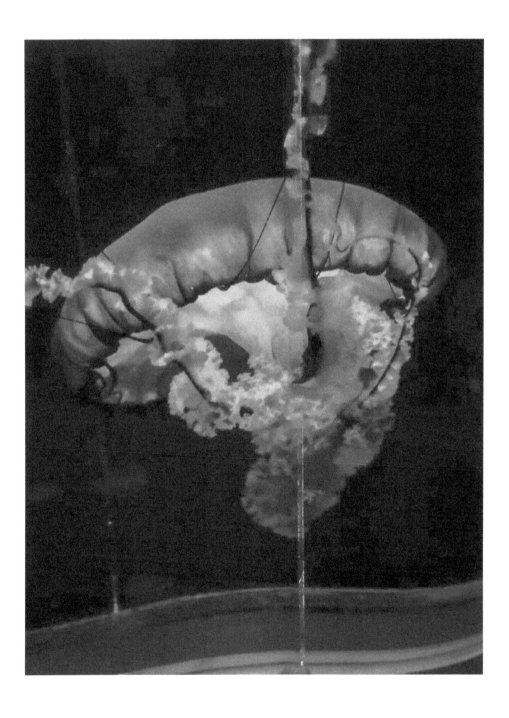

7 Pounds

She said I reminded her of Will Smith

Well she was right because she's the Emily Poss to my Ben

7 pounds of guilt

"What if?"

The game we play to sugar coat the disappointment of life

Running from my pain by giving joy to those who I feel deserves it and deem worthy

Depression

I need an ambulance

Suicide freezes the pain from the jellyfish of life we refuse to untangle ourselves from

An eye for an eye, a heart for a heart

Seven pounds is all it takes to spark a start

I die to have my heart beat for you, eyes like Ezra help me to finally see how a part of me can truly be in her or him, he or she, them, you

Seven strangers touched by seven seconds

Everything Right

Breathe Israel...

inhale

Just

start exhale BREATHE
Finish exhale

You have accomplished
much but it feels like
nothing

You feel stagnant

As if your spirit animal were
that tireless hamster

Running...And running...
AND RUNNING...on the
wheel to nowhere

Doing everything it can
to reach the immediate
intangible goal known as
destiny

You don't even know what it
is fully

Like a hazy distant memory
you try and try and try
to recall exactly what it

is you know your heart is
supposed to do

Be

Have

Know

Grow

Growing...

Growing weary from doubt
are you Iz?

You're like flash if he
never ate

Your hunger for victory
precedes your crippling
dependency

Your energy source you run
from

Not everyone is meant to be
a hero and save the day the
way you do

You're different

Everyone knows it

Everyone reminds you

But you don't see it

You stifle the belief with the self-concept of being sub-par

But you're playing golf my friend

Even when you try to lose you win

Now calm down I'm only telling you what you need to hear

Not what you think you know

I love you

Israel, I love you

Say it loud

Scream it even because self love to you is uncomfortable

To you you treat yourself like an ex that ripped your heart out

You deny their existence so heavily

So aggressively

So maliciously

start yelling

Because they knew what they DID!!!

They hurt you, you know it, they know, EVERYONE KNOWS IT!

You did everything right! EVERYTHING RIGHT!

Who knew words could hurt so much!

I'm not a bitch

But all of me wants to remember that she was

She betrayed you

Your LOVE

Your TRUST

Your RESPECT

She killed you

I guess it's not so bad dying a second time

You died once before Israel

Don't you remember?

You died the day you woke up and realized that the love of your life was gone

With the snap of a finger

No explanation

No remorse

No affection

No twinkle left in his eye

He didn't give a damn!

HOW YOU FELT!

At the mature age of nine, you remember that it was all your fault

It had to be your fault Israel

Why else would your idol be so upset with you?

Manipulation was his tactic

The older you've become you fear he might have picked up a thing or two from mother

My mother, not his

I think she was a great teacher

But I learned the wrong lessons

Laying waste to every vessel I let get close to me

I really am good...I promise

I'm so good I warn you of my habits before you can even feel the pain of each blow

That's how I love myself

I beat the shit out of me emotionally and say get up... if you can't take it then shut the fuck up

My self-talk is a reverse reflection of what I crave

Love

Proper love

Love that no one else can give me

Self-Love

If I were a Phoenix I'd say love just might be my reality of death

I can only experience it after immense pain

And once attained I must let go of it to be reborn again into the monster I've dreaded facing in the mirror

If Jean is my heartbeat then I claw at myself like Wolverine

I let so few people in you'd have to regenerate as you hold me

Most who have made it through have names that start with J

Jesus being first

I don't know how or why

But Reverse Introversion did a number on me

Vulnerability

A concept I find difficult but I'm growing fond of

I don't wanna be like this

Weighing you down with everything I've bottled up inside but it's what's worked best so far

But life has shaken me up and healing thrown in me like a mento

All of the sweet darkness inside me I felt so close to

The hate

The anger

The pain

The uncontrollable circumstances I encountered

Gone

An empty glass bottle, once filled with addictive death no longer

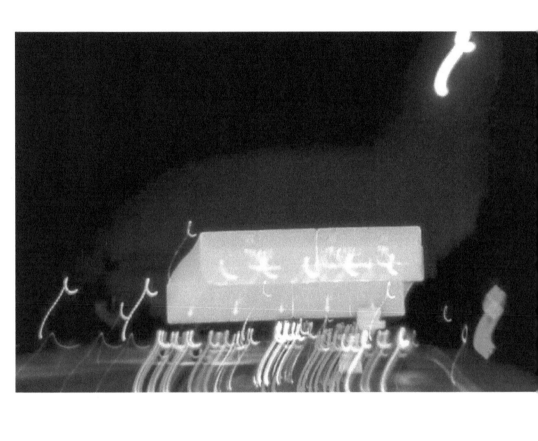

Bloodshot Eyes

Longing

Longing for the moment when I can fall asleep with no regrets

It would be nice to have my eyelids meet for a prolonged kiss while my mind wonders

Forming dreams that would make James Cameron jealous or Michael Bay explode

But I don't dream anymore

I lay facing a screen dreading the moment I fall asleep

I fight my tired soul with a vigor and stubbornness only my closest friends would know I possess

I'm not at peace

I'm restless deeply needing a long night's rest, but the less I rest I prolong a midnight

address, nevertheless, I press my head against my pillow and undress my soul with each recent memory of right and wrong captured by my mouth, ears, and eyes

The gateway but not the only way to the soul

As a hard-nosed

investigator, I scour through the highlife reel of my day marking every moment of imperfection and sinful misdeeds

Reckless endangerment, negligence, and violation of basic self-care are all charges

"Guilty!" I yell, not with words but with lack of sleep, I rest my case

But I can't stop longing

Do I long out of fear

Fear of perpetual loneliness

Do I long out of want?

Wanting to feel the heart of another next to mine

Or do I long out of both?

Fear of wanting someone, needing someone, trusting someone else

I swear I need therapy

I'm losing my mind over something that links to a deeper part of me... potentially a darker side

Not knowing leaves my eyes open wide with eyelids longing...longing to meet again

An Imperfect Cycle

I guess my parents could sit
and ask themselves where
they went wrong

How their son turned out to
be the way he is

Distant

Aloof

Roaming

Wandering

Through life from one
experience to the next

Never stopping to ask them
for help

Guidance

Advice

Assurance

Hope

Hope that in the mess of a
life it gets better

I feel like I lost that

The pain of taking one step
after the other became
immensely unbearable

The burden of life is always
heaviest when one carries it
alone

We weren't designed to grow
strong enough to carry it on
our own

Life adapts to you like a
never ending game of chess

Your strengths its primary
target

It learns your technique
and makes the necessary
adjustments to keep you
guessing

Keep you learning

Keep you growing

My growth takes me on a
journey all its own

Leaving me wandering

Roaming

Aloof

Distant

Alone

With my parents no longer asking but telling me...you didn't get it wrong

There's no one to fully blame

We're just human...and so are you

And so it loops

Like a never ending realization

Breaking habits are like...

Never stopping to ask them for help

Guidance

Advice

Assurance

Hope

Hope that in the mess of a life it gets better

I feel like I lost that

The pain of taking one step after the other became immensely unbearable

The burden of life is always heaviest when one carries it alone

Wait this sounds familiar

Skipping

Skipping

Skipped

Ah yes, I was just about to say...

Breaking habits are like someone pausing your favorite song right after you yell "THIS IS MY PART RIGHT HERE!"

Stopping just shy of the long awaited breakout moment

Rude is what it is

Excruciating, actually, probably fits better

Because we all need to cope

And everyone has theirs tucked away somewhere they think no one can find it

Funny thing is everyone sees it

If not before, now

If not now, eventually

If not eventually, then the future is an asshole that

God allowed to naturally select who would be perfect a part from Jesus

What's done in the dark WILL come to light

Honesty is bliss

Blisteringly painful at first but rewarding in the long run

The marathon

The race to perfection never ends...death is only the commercial break

Stay tuned for more after...

And so it loops

Like a never ending realization

Your growth takes you on a journey all its own

Leaving you alone

Distant

Aloof

Roaming

Wandering

Don't let the redundancy of life's lessons make you feel like you didn't get anywhere

There's no one to fully blame for current discomfort

I'm just human...and so are you

Giants Can Hide

I can't wait for the day I graduate from the boy who cried wolf

Looking for importance from the things I say before finishing what I do

I do too much moving in silent not even courage the cowardly dog would get spooked

You can't hide what can be seen from a mile away

But you can hide behind it your fears and in its shadow remain invisible

No one ever praises a silhouette of something already breathtaking

But everything is beautiful within its own context

I think I just might be too scared to accept mine

Playing con to the life text scripted for me

Trying to erase something beautiful

But the more paint I throw on it the more character it gets

It's like the world accepts me more when I charge towards life K.O after K.O. after K.O.

You know they say boxing is a dance

Life for me has always been one step ahead

Floating like a butterfly and stinging like a bee

The ring my canvas and my blood, sweat, and tears, its paint

This masterpiece will be one of a kind

I've put too much in it to leave this earth with anything less

Con

Con

Contemplate

Contemplation

as I sit on this couch I look for things inside myself that I have left still packed

Suitcase filled with baggage from my last trip to the planet of commitment

Space traveling so that our worlds don't collide again too soon

My cheeks are no longer Redding from California sunshine

But rather slowly remembering how to truly smile again, with a smile so full thanksgiving would be jealous

My heart beats offbeat like J Dilla my drunken soul still finds rhythm in the chaos

of undiscovered dimensions found in the galaxy of growth and change

Z-stars to DC graph T's Walmart

Raised me until I could afford to love nikes

Sleep eyes, Cheap parts

Picked on, hurt hearts

My emotions feel like a broken record, I'm tired of flipping it over expecting to hear something new

It pops and cracks at every misguided needle hand whose touch jumps the vinyl of my healing rotation

I'm a scratched CD so don't get upset if I skip every now and then

It's not on purpose, but I'm just glad you listened long enough to know the songs of my heart on this album called life

Its spin rotates...

It continues

Rhythm & Blues

If it were a palate you'd find my life spread out in many hues

What to paint next

My latest masterpiece was too absolute to continue yet too abstract to complete

A beautiful mess

Painted red and yellow

Each colored brush stroke fighting the lines of the other with utter stubbornness and intentionally intertwined points of intersection causing visually beautiful chaos

It was forbidden love...

Now thrown into a box

Tucked away

A masterpiece

Unfinished

The second one to date

This metaphor ends here

And so does my contemplation

Contemplate

Con

I conned my way into believing I was a problem

Well I am not a problem, I am honest, truthful, caring, and loving to a fault that is not inadequate but rather to a fault that exceeds human capacity to understand or accept

Con

Confide

Confident

I'm confident that walking this high-wire from one major life moment to another will not end with the gravitational pull of pride waiting to capitalize on one misstep

Off-balanced

Skipped breath

This circus act ends with a plea to stay and rest

One last time

In comfort

Con

Continued

Continuous

Chronological cycle
colliding like waves
crashing on a rocky course

It exhilarates...and if you're
not careful it carries...you
away

Into tempests of
uncontrolled, uncharted,
unknown seas of confusion,
willful ignorance, and
fictitious romance
synonymous with love

Engulfed with genuine...love

Con

Contrast

Contrasting views and
faiths leave colors red and
yellow in a beautiful mess

With tails of red trailing and
wagging in and out of the
chaos

Not by chance

Nor by sheer intentionality

But by spontaneous impulse

It was all abstract

With empty spaces and
unspoken words filling each
space left confusingly clear
to the naked eye

Con

Concept...what a Concept

Generation X...What They Meant To Say

You have to understand that as a black, your odds are illegally stacked against you like contraband, you're culturally boxed and given the key as the door is shut and told you have everything you need to get out.

Don't let the system blame you for its injustice, its incompetence, it's dehumanization, and peace immunizations

Like all diseases, in order to be cured you have to acknowledge that you're sick, little brown boy, little brown girl, remember you are worth loving, you are beautiful, and will continue growing

The power is in your hands to make your dreams come to life, that power is a choice, choose to love yourself first and let the rest unfold

If no one else tells you this, then allow me

I love you for who you were, who you are now, and who you will be

Let God remind you of what He placed inside of you before the creation of man

Young man and young woman, life has already targeted you so remember your training

If you have made it this far, the rode gets harder, but you are more than well enough equipped. Your voice is your biggest world changing attribute. Your pens are instruments to make those words immortal

Let your voice carry on and your writing withstand the test of time and illuminate a map, a path, a journey that takes you towards your success...your destiny...your victory

Trailblazers face what others in their shoes haven't

You are on fire like none other so blaze on and with each step light a fire under those around you

You are enough, which is why you are alive today

Your life, no matter how crazy it may feel, has a purpose

When life pushes you, don't back down, and push back

Stand your ground, if not for you, for those in your situation coming after you

Use your struggle today as your testimony tomorrow

You have that power to shift the tides of normalcy and bring freedom to yourself and those around you

You are a leader, no matter what your parent, uncle, sibling, grandparent, friend, cousin, stepfamily, pastor, teacher, coach, or nation tells you

Let freedom ring, let freedom last, there is freedom in love

Short: Life's Literature

She's deceit disguised as
beauty...
And they wonder why she
calls me a beast
I'm uncontrollable
A force to be reckoned with
Manipulation tactics don't
fool me nah
I think for myself
I study
My library is full of
novels and annotations of
individuals I've studied
Their life spills out on every
page
Might as well have
photographic memory
It helps me predict your
tendency
I've been programmed
to assess hurt and pain
and know all too well its
repercussions
PAIN
Promised
Agony

Inflicted
Nonstop
I didn't discover it but I've
studied it and it's studied me
well
A well of knowledge I draw
from like ink it helps me
create a permanent print on
my life's story
A book I haven't finished yet
but filled with chapters too
painful to revisit I think I've
torn them out and hid them
The frey of papers left
bound to the book missing
the rest of its pages leave
a chilling reminder that to
this life I am bound and am
not complete without those
chapters
The symbolism is almost
foreshadowing
But hope
Still
Casts its light

Mortician

Death

There's so much death in the world

More in this lifetime than I think I can fathom

They say the mind

Our memory

Can only hold but so much... before we start to forget the things of old

Overload

I don't need a shrink to know I'm human

As I shrink into myself...I become less human-more degenerate

I bully myself so that no one else can BEAT me to the punch

The first blow

Self-initiation

Whaling on myself like Willy

I just wanna be free

Have you seen my childhood

I raised myself

Internally

I let no one in

I leave broken pieces of the shattered history I have with those I meet

A pre-assembled ensemble

Starring me

Self-indulgence

Self cruelty

Self-critic

Self-care

Self-indulgence

Obsessed with the best at least I'm self-aware

Enough to know I doubt I'll truly be enough

This isn't the me most see...
but yet...it's a part of me

One day I'll beat it

Just might've been
yesterday

My self monologue a verbal
plot

Starring father and son

Each word an unsolicited
bullet

That makes me Ahmaud
Aubrey

The government, Self
Worth, turns a blind eye

Says nothing

Silent

Until the blood of my youth
cries out and screams loud
enough to be taken serious

Therapy

Justice

Hate starts internally It's
self-indulgent

Death

Wailing on ourselves unable
to be free

There's so much death in the
world

Overload

Love...seems out of place
here

Numb

More in this lifetime than I
think we can fathom

They say the mind

Forgets trauma to protect
the psyche of its host

Our memory

Time

A matter of

Can only hold but so much...
before we start to become
the things of old

The thing we hate

Overload-PAIN

Avoid-ANGER

Avert-SADNESS

Suppress-NO

Address-YES

Override-SELF

Death-NOTHING

Leave-*SILENCE*

Love

Missing Bay

These seas they swim

Through rocks and pockets
of time, there's no sublime to
explain the fun and fear in
these eyes

As I Will to be

A black Smith, fresh prince,
Syre, Sirens, things to wake
me up from the sirons

I-Am

An

I-con

Living

This is America

Nah that's childish

I'm no longer a child

In America

Not a Greek myth but like
Odysseus my ship carries
me on

Traveling the world has
been so strange,

Songs swim through these
ears leaving sands of
memories to dry on the skin
tissues of my brain

Rock Rock Rickety Rock
went the Tick Tock Tickety
Tock clock on the wall far
from its shores guiding the
captains' hands home

First strangers now make
the crew, Lovin the Crew
not just on the weeks' ends

There's no chance that
rappers could think about
blessings falling in their laps
like this

(N-N-Neh-Neh-
Neh, -N-N-Neh-Neh-Neh,

Yaaaa-c!)

Cigarettes...

Excuse me, Charlotte was
a girl I knew from birth to
16, she was a queen, yes I

don't regret the things she told me

It seems that supreme is not just a bag with white words but a pizza with white sauce...the sauce always lasts longer than the juice

Because the sauce, the sauce is forever

Best Buy that knowledge for free from Instagram

College ain't free like loaders who think they fam

They were, before the eye could see that their mind's eye had cataracts making them blind to loyalty and reality

These words they sink into the deep dark crevasses of your soul like the titanic, memories aren't determined by what you saw or heard as much as by what you felt

In here(taps heart)

Vietnam I feel you and know that I will see you again one day

As the sea becomes breezy I can't help but say, there's never a right time to say goodbye

We-onna-boat(Rihana) hit by the Chris-p taste of an alcohol-free smoothie(wink), like fist to face, we rock back and forth

Looking, and watching as the jellyfish of life reminds us mortals that it stings even if you are paying attention

I swam these seas and talked to it's dragons. It's breath scorching, leaving a thickness and humidity unlike any other

As I took off the shores I yelled up to the sky's that I had to depart, the dragons descended and asked me Hoi Long

Lilacs from a Mother

Today I woke up to the whispers of someone I knew but never heard speak

It was like finally hearing your dog or cat speak for the first time, you've imagined how they'd sound

Who wouldn't

They're friends to us in time of need

But the whisperer told me that she was dying

Talk about pillow talk

This was heavy

It was earth

THE. Earth.

Mother Earth

She told me that she feels no one listens to her

Yes environmentalists do but they put words in her mouth...slightly bending the truth

And others, she said, ignore her and abuse her as if she had no say in her future

She told me she...

She tried to contain the first signs of the virus...the first cough

But every uprooted tree, displaced flower, water redirected and eternally damned tied her hands behind her back unbeknownst to the ignorant

She can do nothing but watch humanity take the blow

Her tone was apologetic... empathetic even but she never once admitted taking responsibility

I knew it wasn't her fault... she was just caught in the cross-hairs

Collateral damage to a physically phenomenal pandemic piloting perceived perjury

Man vs. man

She told me she had a cure but it's revelation can only come at the hands of those who find it

She told me in the mean time to tell the world that, although they're selfishly engaged with their lives gripped by fear, she just wanted the best for mankind

She's seen something like this before

Countless times even and told me she found that love was the closest thing to a physical cure

The silver lining to the end of a story...her story

She stopped speaking

I opened my eyes to what I thought was a dream only to find a Lilac flower lovingly laid on the other pillow next to me

It was both a sign and a message

I took botany in high school so I knew

Lilacs symbolize love

A newfound love and the first love between mother and child

This was a message...a seed I wish to replant

Hopefully, these words find fertile soil

Jester

There was a queen once.
I was stimulated by her
power, seduced by her
crown, left mute with her
stare, deaf and dumb by her
smile
But it could never be
No
I was just a jester, her
jokester
The one dedicated to put a
smile on her face
I knew her
Better than any prince or
king
I knew what she liked...what
she loved...what she hated, I
knew
I've learned!
But it didn't matter
I was just her jester a few
feet from her scepter but
never close enough to carry
the weight with her
With my queen

She'd have me in her private
quarters only to shift her
thoughts from a bad dream
I was there when she needed
someone most
I told her riddles and
narrated stories of old filled
with nursery rhymes and
forbidden love
She loved those most
Stories of forbidden love
She told me she wished she
could tell jokes as I had
She doesn't give herself
enough credit
But she trusts me, more
than she will any other man
I'm protective, and with her
permission, will ardently
protect her until the end of
time
I'll do anything for my
queen...I would do anything

Head & Heart

My mind told my heart it was smarter and therefore knew the most about love

My heart laughs and then states shortly after that it doubted love would agree because to understand love best is to feel it

My mind placed a bet that it could survive without my heart

Petty

My heart said that for my mind to be so smart, that would have to be the dumbest thing on earth

Witty

See, my mind and heart have a cat and mouse relationship

Katty

My mind, like Tom, bullies my heart, like Jerry

My heart like Jerry, outwits my mind, like Tom

One unable to exist without the other

Needy

The perfect counterbalance

They never talk to one another...the music does that for them

I wish my heart and mind talked more...

But I've come to learn that sometimes more...is less

Mental stress at its best leaves my heart in a dismembered mess

Left in the dark, my mind conspires

My heart guards itself, from its unknown desires

The heart a parachute when my mind base jumps to conclusions

A life lived on the ledge
leaves lamenting lacerations

Pain

My heart then arrests
my thoughts with mass
incarceration

Blame

Berating it with feelings of
hurt and negligence

Stain

My heart yells at my
mind that it wished they
never met

Shame

My mind turns from my
heart saying, "I guess more
really is less"

Strain

My heart, filled with
empathy soon regrets what
it said

Apology

I can't love without thinking
of how to be there for others

I can't love without feeling
how to accept myself

Love is thinking and
feeling...love is more...and
more...is less

Black Loss

Loss

Losing happiness

Losing sleep

Losing love

Losing faith...in a system meant for liberty and justice for all

Who have privilege

Three words blind copied on the pledge of allegiance

Not much has changed since Native Americans met smallpox

A foreign plague to their homeland

Smallpox, sorry I meant Pilgrims

Manipulative hypocrites

Evolved to now be known as politicians

Every vulture has a left and right wing

Picking at the lives of the living until dead

Eagles the only vested predator

Heartbreak

An interruption to all the noise

Death

Permanent release of a human's life

Love

Can either break the cycle or repeat back to heartbreak

Black Lives Matter...

I've been quiet

Silent

My thoughts reaching new depths

My heart trying to catch up with my breaths

Death only eight minutes and forty-six seconds away

I'm evolving

Revolving thoughts revolutionizing resilience towards disruption

I'm hurting

I'm upset

I want to use words but it's not easy when English is all I know

A white language

Structured in close resemblance to history and slavery

It's funny how a noun and a verb are always in the same sentence but one always does the work

Noun- to describe a person, place, or thing

Change(n.)- the act, process, or result of changing

As a noun, this word has not done much for me, a black man in America

The act: has gone on since 1862 and 1964

Process: has been intentional racism and discrimination since slavery

Result of changing: N O T H I N G...but inciting continued oppression

But every noun needs a verb...or maybe 3/5's of one might do

Verb- to describe an action, state, or occurrence

Black American verbs have always had to fulfill the work and action of the white American nouns

The make or break of every sentence resting on the back of verbs

WHITE AMERICAN IGNORANCE MUST CHANGE

Not as a noun but as a verb

Now it's time to rewrite and unlearn

To challenge and restructure

To not just classify but demonstrate change

Change(v.)- to make radically different/to make a shift from one to the other

This is for the privileged

Those unable to acknowledge or speak out against the realness of racism, discrimination, hate crimes, or why black lives seem to only matter when

in the same breathe as that which is fecal

White America

A human centipede of self righteous degradation

A constipated train of thought blocked by the internal rejection and indigestion of owning white privilege

There is no more sympathy for white fragility

Dear white people

Apologies are not enough

Reposts are not enough

Dating someone of color is not enough

Calling other white people racist is

N O T

E N O U G H

DO YOUR RESEARCH AND USE WHITE PRIVILEGE TO HELP ACTUALLY CHANGE THIS BROKEN SYSTEM FUELED BY RACIAL INEQUALITY AND INEQUITY

Learn how race began

What race does TO Black Americans and what race does FOR White America

Research what it means to have white privilege

Vote for candidates who are openly anti-racism in practice and community involvement

I'm sorry in advance if they're not republican

Be uncomfortable

If you are not uneasy or uncomfortable about what you learn then dig deeper and push harder towards truth

Because the truth is uncomfortable when it challenges your false reality

Search for truth

Which is an ACTION

And I promise, you will learn how to better love(v.s)

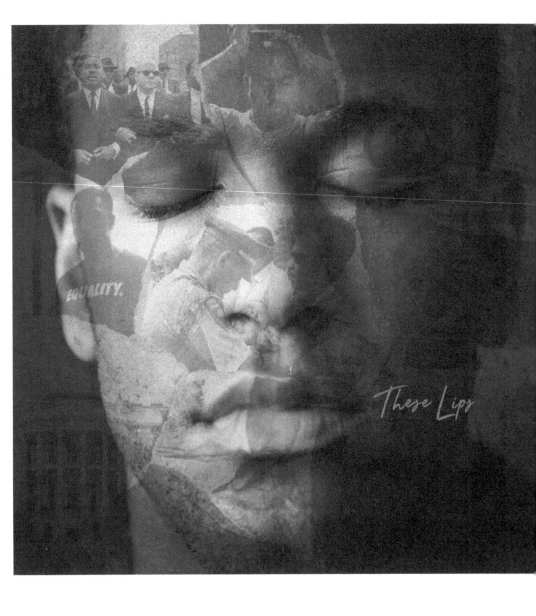

These Lips

These Lips

Living in a world where honesty is weakness

I try to speak to a beat but those drums are useless

I just want to impress you so you know that I'm a wordsmith

With these lips

But there's something about just speaking

A poet knows their lane

Without lines to mark or confine I'm free and no longer a prisoner to the ways of silence

Hands up don't shoot

Violence

Suppressed emotion and insecurity

Anger

Hurt me so I'll never be hurt again

Bitterness

Too late for forgiveness

This pain is too much to live with

Father can you hear this?

How much of our tomorrow do we really have?

About enough to hold in a woman's back pocket

Women don't have them... just to clarify

Curves on display,

Shame, shame, shame!

Chill...she just chose comfort today

I'm a bell boy, well a bell man

In a whiter-land known as The Allison

You a black boy, where yo J's then?

You a black girl, put your weave in

The higher up the more white it gets

Cumulus clouds from the ground look full but when in the midst of it, it's emptiness wreaks of jealousy

Jealousy of the cultures and traditions that exist below

I guess, now I know that's where we get fog from

Thick clouds descending from the nines on high

Ironic how something so high can stoop so low

Manipulating reality and distorting perception

Causing collisions from lack of foresight and white interference with elections

I'm just a prophet, well a poet

And you should know dat

I'm no politician but I know my rights

Freedom of speech

Not really cuz I gotta keep it PC

We

Idolize

Ideologies and idiosyncrasies of the state forcing truth of our nations ugliness to be nipped and tucked, broken and cut, laced and poured in, a bottle of privilege, where race was born an

I'm tired of white belligerents high key

My thoughts shift in a swoosh

Checking that box: still buying nikes

Blackkklansman

Get Out

Narratives of minority life giving us a voice

Kanye in the sunken place sounding like Ron Stallworth, "slavery was a choice"

I guess Ye ready to die to Make America Great Again

Ye versus the people, sleeper, WAKE UP YE before you get got by the reaper

Sometimes we're not sleep but just in shock from the secretive chaos now seen

This world just keeps getting scarier

I sound like I never saw this coming but it sucks to know that your worst nightmares are your everyday reality

We need a new President

Somebody might shoot me because I'm speaking truth

I'm a black man

I'm not allowed to fail and that's a lot of pressure. I can't mess up or else I lose it all...

Which sucks the life out of determination to try

But I guess the system was never broken, it's just serving its purpose as the system that's working perfectly

MLK knew his time was near because of the gifts and passions he held inside...I guess I do too

I'm tired of living in a world where honesty is weakness

Imma speak my truth!

Cuz

White America has brought me so much pain

Depression...intercession, joy regression...for my lack of confessin

I've been angry,

Running and sitting, crying and sniffing, my inner thoughts holding me hostage with murdered ambition

I've been tired of failing, tired of faking, tired of living, tired of making, mad at the world, tired of giving, the only parts of me left sacred and livin

America

A world where the hate you give suffocates a Starr

Imma speak to this beat while my words remain ruthless

I'm not a rapper I'm wordsmith

With these lips

Silent Pillows

The room has gotten colder

The stars twinkle red, green, and orange

No light pollution to quiet the darkness that is the ceiling

Technology's soft glow replacing natural light

A bed meant for two in love replaced with two in pain

Minimal robotic movements made by each as if to pretend the enemy closes in and neither can make a sound

A game of red light green light gone wrong

The game-master, cupid, fell asleep with the last command as red

Blinded by love...his own two eye-lids

Ironic being that I can't close my eyes and neither can she

I don't know for sure

But part of me hopes she cares too

That her heart beat radiates its thump to her temple as it is doing mine

I hope she too feels the temperature of the room drop

Like I did, hit by the tranquilizer of questioned loyalty

My orientation lost in the ravine that splits right down the middle of our king sized bed

She's so close I can hear her breathe, yet so far I fear I might not make the journey

I fear caring more

Wanting more

Hoping for more

Fighting for more

Maturing more

But what if more is too much

It was

My life taught me not to ever push too far past what it gives you

Rejecting the hand that feeds you expecting more is almost the same as biting it

Trust me, I've learned

Yet, is this truly what I learned or am I confusing lessons?

Applying algebraic algorithms to philosophical theory?

Attributing my limited understanding to that which surpasses the aptitude of mankind

Complicating something simple or simplifying that which is eternally complicated

Entanglement

I am disoriented and all I want is for this all to end

Maturity sets in

Ego loses and humility wins

So I reach for her

Credits roll

The end

Trees and Routes

If trees had voices, there are
a few who'd call me by name

My route to and from
home is sometimes largely
dependent on my mood

On good days

I leave home in just enough
time to arrive at my
destination quickly

That's a walk down the
street, and a hop on the max
line heading downtown

Typically close enough to
my stop for me to just turn a
corner or two

My ear-buds in, no they're
not air-pods, I'm not a
conformist

Which is why I'm listening
to Sir The Baptist

Saint or Sinner

Ever heard of him?

Anyways, I'm an albums guy

Again, nonconformist

But each tree I pass on this
route is welcomed with a
smile and appreciation

On neutral days

I still leave my home in just
enough time to arrive to my
destination quicker...or I
guess I just leave later

The only difference is, this
time I'm listening to Jon
Bellion

The Human Condition

My eyes no longer admiring
each tree passed with
excitement but rather subtle
melancholy

It's more subconscious than
conscious, because I promise
If you asked how I was

I'd smile as if disrupted
from a deep thought and
say, "I'm good!"

And fully believe it...

My eyes never lie

The trees

On this route

Have a better understanding of what's going on

Beneath the surface of my smile within the soil of my heart

Trees know that this is where death starts

Beneath the surface

Our root, determines our destination

Whether we get there or not

On bad days

I don't want to leave my home...my room...my bed... my sleep...or dreams...even if they're nightmares

Because at least, then, my emotions can run free and not constantly inflict on me a sense of purgatory

My trees

Nature's cornerstone

Can't find me

I don't make it out to the great beyond that day

Self care day

A very rare day

But a watering day

The roots of my heart and soul run dry

Empty

Empty of life...much like my routes in the outside world

Running empty of life

Today

These days

Even now

On good days, neutral, and sad days my trees miss me... and I miss them

My routes

Filled with roots

Whose whistling voices sing my name to the melodic tunes of Sparrows, Finches, and Flickers have want of company

I know that feeling

Feeling lonely

So I listen

Not with air-pods, headphones, or headsets

But with the very things God made me

My uncovered ears

I put nature's album on repeat, every time I open my window

To the outside world

Therapy

With this I reminisce on the days I miss

The days I existed among the trees

Sessions

Sharing with each the secrets that exist beyond my eyes... beneath the surface...at roots of my heart

Reaching Forever

Photos haunting me

Emotions attached

Even so

I detach from the idea of
who you were

Who we were

Seeing doubles of you, never
quite getting to why you're
now a forever Ex

I won't apologize for saying
goodbye

There's only room for one in
my heart

I know that our
moment was...

Just that

A blink in time with no need
to rewind

I don't hate you, it's out with
the old and in with the new

Or better put, you still have
a hold and without you I
gotta move through life

Pull through

For me

For her

For us

Wife

My future family

I'm thinking marriage see

My left hand losing touch,
like gollum, reality doesn't
exist without something
precious

My precious

She reminds me I'm Sméagol

Killing my servility for
everyone but her

Voices from above guiding
me like Frodo

I'm lost without her

Whether North or South
she's still my Carolina

Her words bandage my
wounds, her ears catch

every cry, her heart carries every suitcase

Knowing what's inside is filled with those before

Trust

She doesn't peak

Calls me boo

There's no hiding from her

From you

My future

There's no going back, lust set aside like a Delorian

Tempting me to revisit moments that were meant to be left alone

Timelines

Lifelines

No regrets

No remembrance

No sadness

Eternal happiness caught in the present rewritings of past imaginations

How can you respond to a timeline that could have been but that will never be?

Choice

I bury my past fantasies like Tony Stark

End Game

Internal World Peace

Deuces

I used to sound like Confucius making up excuses

For why I couldn't let go of who you were to me

Didn't want to become the self fulfilling prophet, walking away from someone who loved me

Like someone first did to me

That feeling hits different

Hole in the wall

The fist of a lover leaving

Blindsided

The wall, my heart pre Fort Knox

Guarded

I stopped believing in love until I met you

Grappling with to be and not to be's

Now looking for a settlement

A family to create a Hamlet   Just a perfect reflection...of

Tragedy is a life without you   Y

Now when you look at me   O

In my eyes   U

You don't see them   That just leaves me...and
you...forever

Self-Disclosure

Self-Disclosure

Pocket dials at 11 FaceTime calls at midnight

Mid flight, because my dreams were takin off to new heights

REM sleep, space heat, sweat leaks, from widows peak, wool blanket from skinned sheep, that's love goin skin deep, brrr-brrr, lil black me, is you willing to freeze as His sheep

Attack sneak, reverse shriek, Lil bo-peep

Them toys freak, when Sid creeps, creative or savage, that kids not average, we all got baggage, as hoarders we salvage, and manage to package our damage in passage, to not be weak and get taken advantage

Of, piquing interest always risks adage, I'm fragile, in love, not in hate, gifts are the worst

Don't take them as bait

Don't label me fake, cuz then you mistake

Me

For a man that hasn't seen, a man that hasn't heard, a man that hasn't lived in a world that doesn't turn the other cheek

Seven times seventy, sometimes I wish I skipped math, counting forgiveness is counting your freedom, long life and longevity putting you on a path to hear and heed, so lead em

I'm not perfect, with chink in my armor and targets on my back, I didn't ask to be me but I guess we never choose, so I take a step back, reflect on my humanity

89

and then I go back, to the start when I realized that every Mr. Perfect has imperfections

Lust vs Love has been my lifelong fight

Young wild and free, young dumb and broke, feelin old but I'm young, feelin cold cuz I'm stuck

In guilt

These episodes are random but in tandem with my first exposure to porn

This then became the new male standard

I was floored, sex educated, and prematurely coming to my own idea of love

My teacher reluctantly telling me about birds, bees, and condemns

I was homeschooled...

As you can imagine the conversation was mad awkward and tense, crash course on anatomy was now past tense, Victoria's angels had to be heaven sent

Of this I was convinced but repented, repeatedly, relapsing establishing sinful happenings

At 14 lack of innocence was a mystery, until my folks discovered my google history, that's when guilt began to notice me

Coke and mentos weren't my type of bottle rockets

Room door lock it

Hard?

Well sock it

Heart might pop at

Any stroke an

just might die cuz, mom just walked in an

We all have been there

Deny your sin, then

Repeat the offense a-, gain, and again, an

This is how it starts, men turn out like Kevin's Hart, J Cole K.O.D. forget a dolla, how much does a woman cost?

I don't mean no disrespect, it was a point to just address

and resurrect the inspection into the conviction of males lack of self-control, we need an intervention

Male privilege times insecurity plus natural instinct times hypermasculinity equals self-entitled sexual dependency

Jeepers keepers, away from creepers, horn dogs as heat seekers, target acquired, quick blast offs demean her

Women

She takes it all to the face and calls it value, doesn't even argue, she just wants to make you happy and feel like she's loved by you

We all have wants and we all have needs, sacrifice

is relationship with the absence of greed

Love is different than lust, nuts actually were meant to bust, but not at the expense of another's unconditional trust

Vulnerability breaks the cycle

Self-disclosures and internal explorations leave explanations for current emotional expectations, so women we need a safe place and men they need better communication

Let me hop off the soap box

Bet

You caught me preachin

Self-disclosure

I'm still in therapy

Let my thoughts scroll

Dreaming of Death

Adulthood, marketed a false show

Stable hearts fall in love too slow

I don't know

Who to expect next

What to expect when love gets undressed

Shows scars from bedrooms of unrest

A sexual express

Like a shot of expresso

An expression of how to let go

And fall

Like a loss at limbo

Dying an endless death
to give life to another you barely know

Two worlds colliding
shouldn't try to stay whole
avoiding commitment, no

It's give and take

Apologies and grace

Break down and remake

Break away and excavate

The layers of old

Strip your planets to the very core

Circling the center, molten rocks sizzle

With boulders hardened from pain and grief

But just beyond the barrage of self protection

For the strong who dig a little deeper

You'll find the never ending light that resides within

In you

In us

As two

Becoming one

Infused

Two balls of fire burning

Melting

Together

Underneath the stars uncovered in the cauldron of metaphorical nakedness

I never said this process was pretty

It takes time

It's never short of beauty

Love's crime

Earth didn't start with a boom, birth was created from the first bang

A big bang

I wouldn't know

Wasn't there

Don't care

Humans shouldn't wear underwear

We should just lay bare

Untouched by the fear of vulnerability and openness

Left to the solicited touch of truth

A masseuse who gets the knot out every time

A bruise, left to remind you that healing takes time

Don't irritate it

Let it be what it is without dispute

Just rest

Rest in the arms of the imperfect

And die a death that awakes you in your dreams

All for another

Love's true crime, a story about the first time of forever that I died for her

My lover

God Gave Me You

I write to you with love
flowing ever so freely

This is to you, beautiful

The one who's hair is so
well kept you are your
hair stylists favorite and
quickest head

Your forehead creates
wrinkles so soft and elegant
you make man made play-
doh jealous

Your eyebrows bend up so
that the arrow of your pupil
darts towards it's intended
target

Bulls-eye

You see and notice
everything

You speak with them,
your soft, warm eyes filled
with endless emotion and
conversation that spill from
the brim

Your nose, the perfect
bridge with nostrils who's
flair taunts more than Rick
himself

And those cheeks, create
canyons of acceptance as
it meets the curve of your
breathtaking smile

You killer you

The things you do to people

Men and women alike

It's dangerously unfair

This is to you, humanitarian

Oozing with charisma
coupled with care you give
me a run for my money too
often

You get me in trouble with
you at times

This is to you, goofy

The one who's laugh fills
a room even if the joke
wasn't that funny...mmmm

because you thought of something clever to respond and couldn't get it out quick enough

Oh and not to mention your tones dedicated to sarcasm

There wouldn't be a you without it

This is to you, oh serious one

The one who sits through agonizing conversations because you know the power of listening and compassion

Claiming and owning every fault of yours and the others'

Whether it sisters, cousins, brothers, aunts, or mothers

You stay, you listen, you joke, you smile, you cry, you are there

This is to you, the muted one

The one who allows your insecurities to leave you silent when people need to hear you most

Not to help themselves but for them to be there for you

When you hide behind your smile, or a joke, or someone else's pain

When you push aside the truth and knowingly trade them for lies

Despise

I despise when you do that!

Don't you know your worth!

Don't you know people care!

Don't you know I care, damnit!

This is to you, over-analyzer

The one who gets on my last nerve with your self sabotage

Self-pity

Self-indulgence

Self-correcting

Self-entitling

Self-saving(which is a delusion)

Self-denying(of good things like food, water, and sleep)

Self-criticizing

Need I continue? Because if you are here you know this is for you!

I don't say this cuz I
hate you

I don't

I mean sometimes maybe
but we've talked about
changing that

And you have

Which I have to say I'm
proud of you for

You have grown so so much
this past decade

No I'm serious

out or corner of mouth
Cuz I have stories lemme tell
ya ha

But I won't, cause I
know you private and
everything but

Honestly this is for you, my
forever

The one who I cherish, love,
and adore

To the one who is always
there for me when no one
else is

To the one who helps pick
me up when I'm low...most
times

To the one who claims me
despite my flaws

To the one who has stuck by
my side as long as I can even
remember, protecting me,
loving me, listening to me,
looking out for me

Telling me to stay strong
when I felt I couldn't

For pushing me towards
God when I felt neglected,
misused, abandoned,
and disrespected by the
challenges of life

You stuck with me

So this is for you...Israel Cole
Hammond

To the one I admire and
adore, I write with love ever
so freely

Because I truly love you

I love everything about you

Your Beauty

Your Humanness

Your Goofiness

Your Silence

Your Over-Analyzing

And Dedication to me...to
us(Spirit, Soul, and Body)

You're going to be okay, you're going to make it

You have a heart for God and the world and that's why I love you so much

And even still, you have managed to have a heart for yourself

To be the very best version of yourself

Day in and day out

Pure, Genuine, Raw, and Unfiltered

This is to you my friend, my confidant, my body whom I love dearly beyond every curve, ability, and lack thereof

Thank you, I'm glad you are alive and I am so glad God gave me you